# FANCY DRESS FOR CHILDREN

# FANCY DRESS FOR CHILDREN

## Barbara Snook

## B. T. Batsford Limited

For LAURA

First published 1969
Reprinted 1970

7134 2635 7

Filmset by Keyspools Ltd, Golborne, Lancashire
Printed in Great Britain by
Billing & Sons Ltd, Guildford and London
for the publishers
B. T. Batsford Limited
4 Fitzhardinge Street, London, W1

# CONTENTS

Acknowledgment 7
Introduction 8
PEOPLE—story book, fairy tale, pantomime, nursery rhyme, historical and everyday characters
Alice in Wonderland, The White Rabbit 10
March Hare, White Rabbit Herald 11
Mad Hatter, Dormouse 12
Walrus and Carpenter 13
Red-Riding Hood and Wolf 14
Mermaid 15
Demon King 16
Snow Queen, Snowflake, Fairy Queen 17
Fairy 18
Witch, Wizard 19
Queen of Hearts, Knave of Hearts 20
Jack Sprat and wife 21
Harlequin 22
Columbine 23
Pied Piper 24
Friar Tuck, Robin Hood 25
Bo-Peep, Eighteenth-century lady 26
Miss Muffet, Bo-Peep 27
Tweedle Dum and Tweedle Dee 28
Wee Willie Winkie, Little Jack Horner 29
Jack and the Beanstalk 30
Pirate 31
Jockey, Shepherd 32
Hobby horse, Jousting Knight 33
Dancing Bear and Keeper 34
Jester, Mummer 35
Henry VIII 36
Roman citizen 37
Social Climber 38
Guardsman 39
Chelsea Pensioner, Milkman 40
Nurse, Mrs Mopp 41
Fisherman, Fishy Yarns 42
Daily News, Current Events, Sweep 43
Balloon Seller, Flower Woman 44
Gipsy 45
Indian Brave 46
Squaw 47
Cowboy 48

PEOPLE— *continued*
Eskimo 49
Hawaian Girl 50
Mexican Boy 51
Rajah 52
Indian Woman, Rajah's Page 53
Sheik 54
European Gipsy, Saharan Girl 55
Egyptian Woman 56
Pierrot, Clown 57

OBJECTS— parcels, peculiar things
Boot's Branches 58
Knight of the Bath, Wife of Bath 59
Boxed Goods, Book, Oxo Cube,
    Sugar Bag 60
Alarm clock, Trading stamp 61
Playing cards 62
Christmas Cracker, Cigarette 64
Belisha Beacon, Zebra Crossing 65
Dustbin, Pillar Box 66
Cottage Loaf 67
Saucepan: on the boil; boiling over
    68
Cup of Tea 69
Easter Egg 70
Snowman 71
Bird Table 72
Skeleton 73

NATURE— animals, birds, insects, weather,
seasons
Cat, Rabbit 74
Poodle 75
Bird Masks 76
Bird Wings 77
Cock 78
Hen 79
Dragon 80
Crocodile 81
Tree trunk 82
Ear of Corn 83
Crab 84
Hatching Chick 85
Bumble Bee, Wasp, Butterfly 86
Butterfly, Ladybird, Beetle 87
Rosebud, Daisy 88
Limpet, Seaweed 89
Spring, Summer 90
Autumn, Winter 91
Rain, Water 92
Fire, spark 93
Night and Day 94
Night 95

CONSTRUCTION DETAILS
Animal masks 96

# ACKNOWLEDGMENT

My sincere thanks are due to Miss Linda Cole for her permission to use three bird masks which she designed; to Mrs W. Ellis for once again scrutinizing the manuscript; to Thelma M. Nye for her vigilance at every stage of production; and most of all to Mr Samuel Carr, at whose suggestion the book came into existence.

B. L. S.

Chislehurst 1969

# INTRODUCTION

Almost as soon as the invitation to a fancy dress party falls through the letter box comes the question, 'What shall I be?' or a dogmatic 'I'm going as a paint-box'. Suddenly the old tablecloth that has done duty in so many games of make-believe no longer seems quite adequate for such a special occasion. Soon there are more questions, 'What shall we make it of?' 'How long will it take?', and on the adult level, will it be worn more than once and how much will it cost?

The essence of a successful fancy dress is in its immediate identification. It may be witty, even topical, but never obscure. While an adult may feel complimented by the suggestion of ingenuity implied in the question, 'What are you?' a small child is devastated at not being recognised at once. A pink-tipped daisy who is mistaken for a wild rose, or a coalman for a sweep, may no longer enjoy the party to the full, for want of a little extra time and thought spent on the design.

Choice of costume is not always easy. Popular characters go out of date, topical phrases may last only a few months, slogans such as 'Ship's daily run' interpreted with medicinal salts and toilet paper have a limited appeal even on board a cruise liner.

Current fashion, relied on too much, may result in more fur-hatted Russians and booted cowboys than a party can peacefully accommodate, and fashion in storybook characters can lead to disagreement between one generation and another. A six-year-old can be very scornful about a personage greatly revered by his parent when young.

A child's physique is probably the best guide to success. A very thin little boy will make an excellent pillar box or Pied Piper, whereas he may not turn easily into Henry VIII or even Friar Tuck. The Tournament horse, which is heavy, must be worn by a sturdy boy, and awkward clothes by someone so keen to be a Cottage Loaf or Cup and Saucer that wearing them is amusing and discomfort unimportant. A dress must not be overwhelming . . . if the true proportions of Roman toga and Indian sari are adhered to, such abundant drapery is difficult to handle; far less material will create the right effect. Very young children must wear clothes that come off easily because excitement can cause problems.

It is impossible to make everything of fireproof materials, yet fire is by no means the only hazard. Headdresses in particular, must be made with due regard for everyone's safety—nothing hard or sharp should be allowed to dig into the wearer's head or into that of anyone else nearby in a rough and tumble.

Few clothes in this book need to be made of new material. Everyday clothes, whenever possible, are used as a foundation; shirts, sweaters, jeans, pyjamas, Wellingtons, tights, leotards and dresses. A simple tunic pattern forms the basis of many designs. There is no need to spend hours on beautifully made clothes when just as much pleasure is derived from painted fabric, especially if the wearer can help with paste and paint brush. Buckram is expensive but corrugated cardboard costs little; combined with newspaper and flour paste and covered with old sheeting before being painted, it may be a little heavier but it is certainly stronger. Corrugated paper, pleated, cut and overlapped, stapled or sewn, can be moulded into any shape whether for main garment or mask. Chicken wire, which has many scratchy cut ends difficult to cover even with a lining, should never be used.

Both crêpe paper embellished with a little tempera colour paint applied with the minimum of water and coloured paper cut from newspaper colour supplements and weekly magazines can be put to good use. Various adhesives enable these and small pieces of fabric to be applied to a foundation material. Such devices may considerably reduce cost.

If the whole family co-operates in designing a costume, take care that someone makes sure that it will last throughout the party. Certain materials are flimsy, some games are boisterous, nobody wants to fall to pieces before the time comes to go home.

# ALICE IN WONDERLAND

## WHITE RABBIT

White
leggings

Pompon
sewn between
coat tails

Rabbit cap
see pages 74 and 96

# MARCH HARE

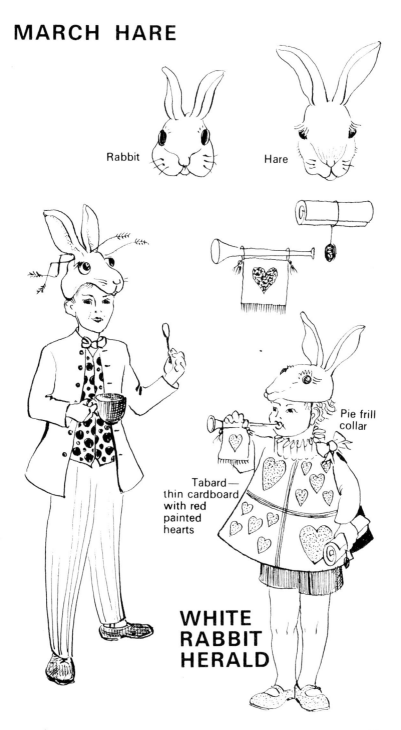

Rabbit

Hare

Pie frill collar

Tabard—thin cardboard with red painted hearts

## WHITE RABBIT HERALD

# MAD HATTER

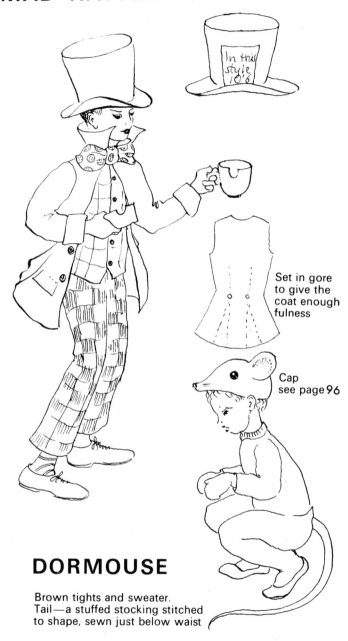

In this style 10/6

Set in gore
to give the
coat enough
fulness

Cap
see page 96

# DORMOUSE

Brown tights and sweater.
Tail—a stuffed stocking stitched
to shape, sewn just below waist

# WALRUS and CARPENTER

Flippers—
Sew stiff
material
on to gloves
or mittens

Baggy
pants

Over-large old
shoes with
stuffed toes

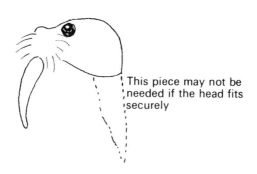

This piece may not be
needed if the head fits
securely

# RED RIDING HOOD
## and the WOLF

Try to use a fur necklet for the
wolf's tail. Tie it to elastic round
the waist and bring through a slit
in the back of the nightie
see Mask, page 96

# MERMAID

Costume for a flaxen child

The colour effect should be silver
grey, grey green, blue green,
deep blue
If sheeting is dyed a mottled blue
green the other colours can be
painted on the scales

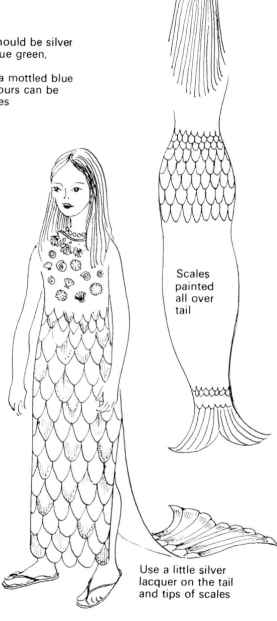

Glue shells to
the bodice

Wear pearl
necklace or
blue green
beads

Blue or green
tights or bare
legs

Scales
painted
all over
tail

Use a little silver
lacquer on the tail
and tips of scales

# DEMON KING

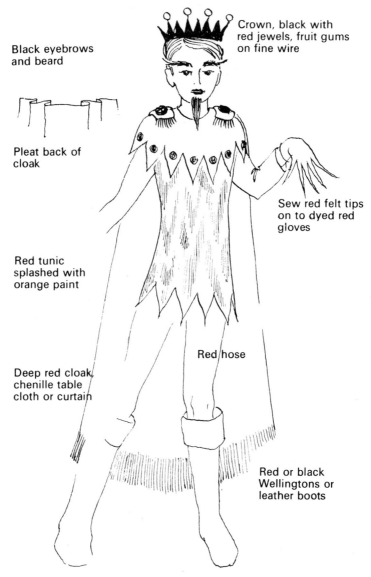

Crown, black with red jewels, fruit gums on fine wire

Black eyebrows and beard

Pleat back of cloak

Sew red felt tips on to dyed red gloves

Red tunic splashed with orange paint

Red hose

Deep red cloak, chenille table cloth or curtain

Red or black Wellingtons or leather boots

Devise a black and red or green and red scheme. A blend of several shades of red and orange or blue green with green will add brilliance to the chief colour

# SNOW QUEEN
# SNOW FLAKE
# FAIRY QUEEN

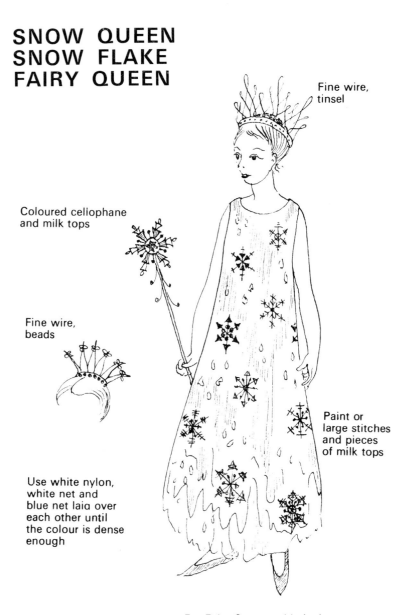

Fine wire, tinsel

Coloured cellophane and milk tops

Fine wire, beads

Use white nylon, white net and blue net laio over each other until the colour is dense enough

Paint or large stitches and pieces of milk tops

Add glitter

For Fairy Queen, add cloak and tiny wings between shoulder blades, if desired

# FAIRY

Twist wire round head-band, glue stars to wire

Padding under bias binding necessary if wire is bumpy

Cut 2 silver paper stars, paste over card, and glue together with the wand in between

Skirt—several gathered layers of net, various shades, not made as a tutu. Matching frilly pants Bodice, net over silk

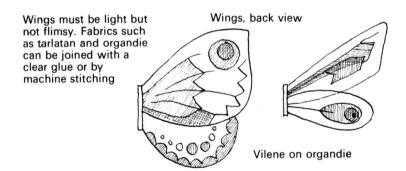

Wings must be light but not flimsy. Fabrics such as tarlatan and organdie can be joined with a clear glue or by machine stitching

Wings, back view

Vilene on organdie

# WITCH or WIZARD

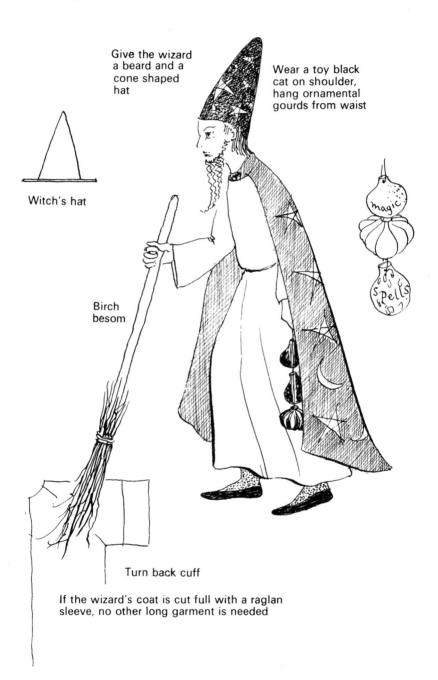

Give the wizard a beard and a cone shaped hat

Wear a toy black cat on shoulder, hang ornamental gourds from waist

Witch's hat

magic

spells

Birch besom

Turn back cuff

If the wizard's coat is cut full with a raglan sleeve, no other long garment is needed

# QUEEN OF HEARTS

Playing card dress
on page 62

Make a heart
shaped red
cloak and
muslin pinafore

Red
hearts
painted
or
applied

White tunic
over black or
red shorts

# KNAVE OF HEARTS

# JACK SPRAT and WIFE

For the judge's procession carry plates with fat and lean meat (painted cardboard)

Padding Sew tapes on to small cushion, cross over and tie in front

# HARLEQUIN

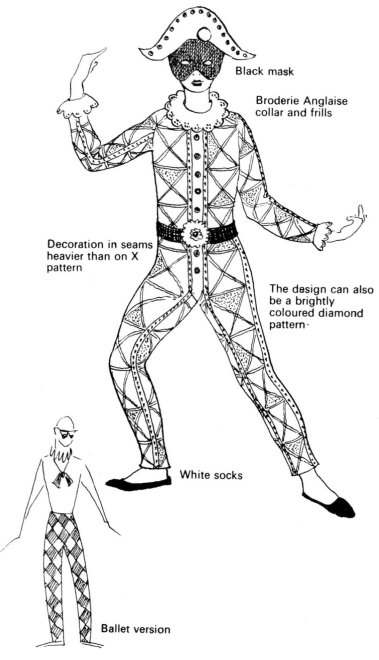

Black mask

Broderie Anglaise
collar and frills

Decoration in seams
heavier than on X
pattern

The design can also
be a brightly
coloured diamond
pattern

White socks

Ballet version

# COLUMBINE

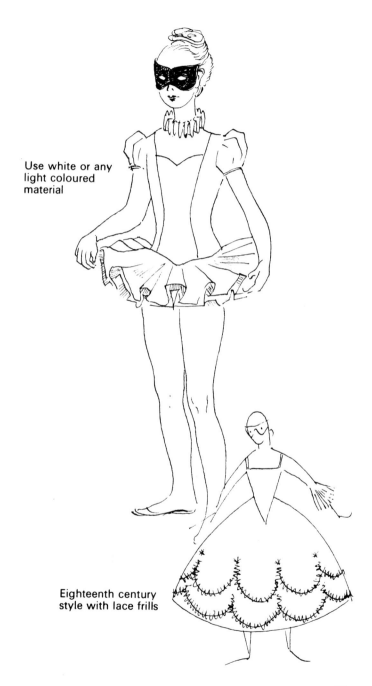

Use white or any light coloured material

Eighteenth century style with lace frills

# PIED PIPER

Cover old
plimsolls
with fabric left
over from tunic

# FRIAR TUCK

Suggest a shorn head by
cutting out a small piece of
flesh-coloured felt held in place
with shirring elastic or clipped to
hair

Brown
habit

ROBIN HOOD can wear a tunic and tights like the Pied Piper, but
made of plain green fabric. He will need a small hat and high
turned-down boots

25

# BO-PEEP

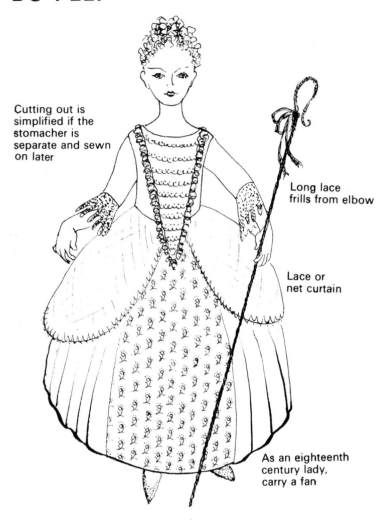

Cutting out is simplified if the stomacher is separate and sewn on later

Long lace frills from elbow

Lace or net curtain

As an eighteenth century lady, carry a fan

An eighteenth century style which could be used, without the crook, as a period costume. Find sprigged or floral brocade for skirt or centre panel, but not for both. Sew lace on stomacher

# MISS MUFFET
## or BO-PEEP

Position of
Miss Muffet's
spider

Make lambs
of Staflex
ironed on to
back of skirt

# MISS
# MUFFET

Back of dress

Make web of long
strands of wool,
the spiders body
of 2 pompons
or stuffed to shape
and its legs of
plaited wool

# TWEEDLEDUM and TWEEDLEDEE

Any child, fat or thin will need padding. Use foam rubber and soft cushions very securely fastened together. Tie over the shoulders, across back and fasten in front. Trousers can be made from oversize pyjamas taken in where necessary

# WEE WILLIE WINKIE

Woollen sock

Remodel an old shirt

# LITTLE JACK HORNER

# JACK AND THE BEANSTALK

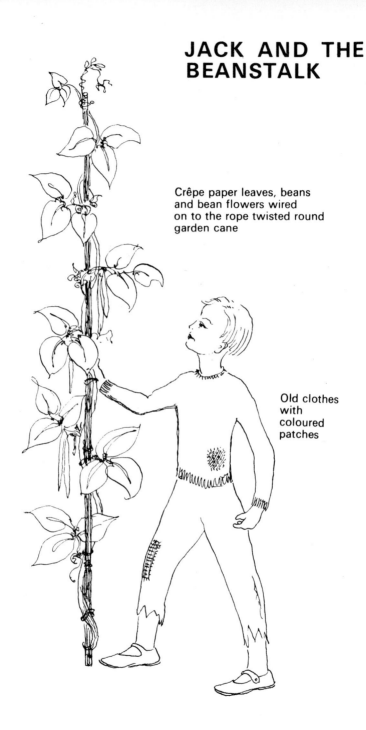

Crêpe paper leaves, beans
and bean flowers wired
on to the rope twisted round
garden cane

Old clothes
with
coloured
patches

# PIRATE

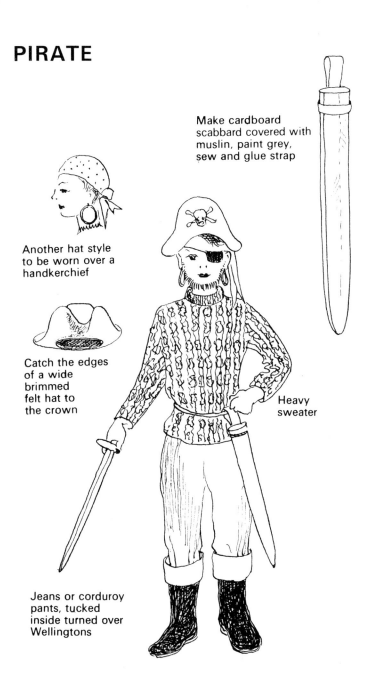

Make cardboard scabbard covered with muslin, paint grey, sew and glue strap

Another hat style to be worn over a handkerchief

Catch the edges of a wide brimmed felt hat to the crown

Heavy sweater

Jeans or corduroy pants, tucked inside turned over Wellingtons

# JOCKEY

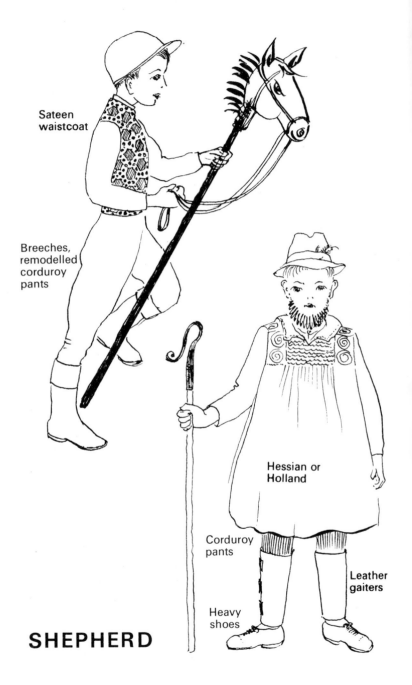

Sateen
waistcoat

Breeches,
remodelled
corduroy
pants

Hessian or
Holland

Corduroy
pants

Leather
gaiters

Heavy
shoes

# SHEPHERD

# HOBBY HORSE

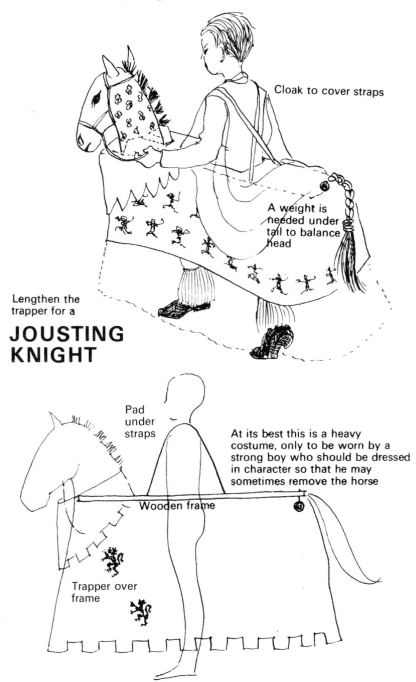

Cloak to cover straps

A weight is needed under tail to balance head

Lengthen the trapper for a

## JOUSTING KNIGHT

Pad under straps

At its best this is a heavy costume, only to be worn by a strong boy who should be dressed in character so that he may sometimes remove the horse

Wooden frame

Trapper over frame

# DANCING BEAR
## and KEEPER

Head construction page 96

Cut bear's skin from a sleeping suit pattern. Use any brown material, on old winter coat if available, corduroy velvet, or fur fabric

Sew rolls of fabric decorated with ribbon on to jacket

# JESTER

Compare with
playing card Joker

White
handkerchief

Black hat with
bright floral garland

Coloured
ribbons

# MUMMER

White jacket
and trousers,
black hat and
shoes, black
shin pads

35

# HENRY VIII

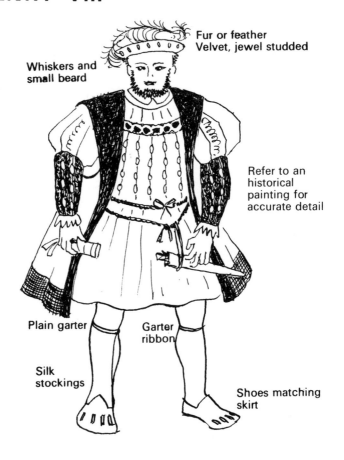

Fur or feather
Velvet, jewel studded

Whiskers and
small beard

Refer to an
historical
painting for
accurate detail

Plain garter

Garter
ribbon

Silk
stockings

Shoes matching
skirt

An elaborate costume best suited to a stocky child. The doublet is slashed, with the white shirt pulled through. The skirt should be made of heavy furnishing fabric, the cloak of some rich material. Extend shoulders with buckram and wadding, cut large armholes in cloak so that the big sleeves can pass through easily

# ROMAN CITIZEN

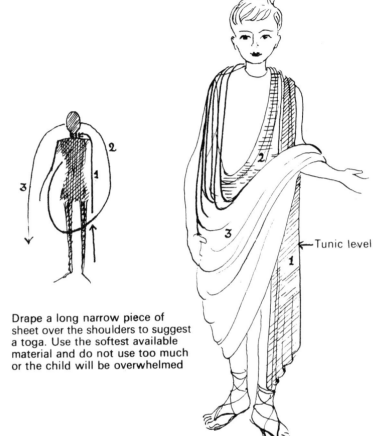

Drape a long narrow piece of
sheet over the shoulders to suggest
a toga. Use the softest available
material and do not use too much
or the child will be overwhelmed

Tunic level

A pattern can be painted round the neck

Julius Caesar wears a wreath

# SOCIAL CLIMBER

Either climbing
breeches or
dark trousers

A mixture of climbing and dress clothes. Wear breeches, shorts or long dark trousers, heavy boots, a dress jacket, tails if possible, bow tie, topper, and carry all the climbing gear obtainable, rope, crampons, ice pick

# GUARDSMAN

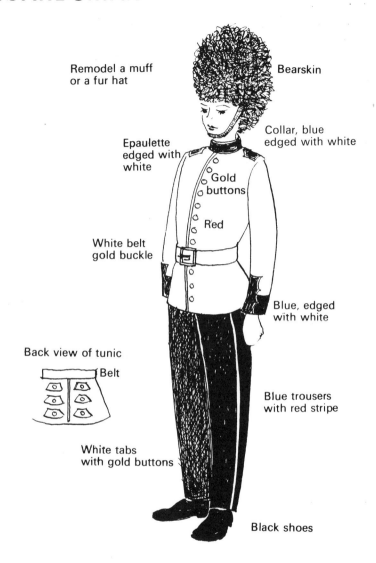

Remodel a muff or a fur hat

Bearskin

Epaulette edged with white

Collar, blue edged with white

Gold buttons

Red

White belt gold buckle

Blue, edged with white

Back view of tunic

Belt

Blue trousers with red stripe

White tabs with gold buttons

Black shoes

# CHELSEA PENSIONER

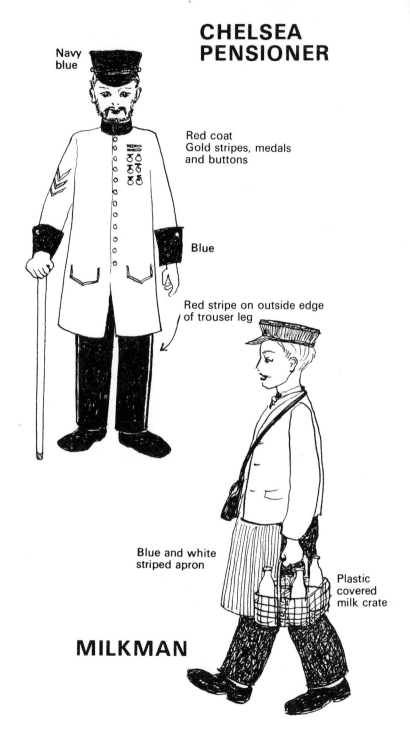

Navy blue

Red coat
Gold stripes, medals
and buttons

Blue

Red stripe on outside edge
of trouser leg

Blue and white
striped apron

Plastic
covered
milk crate

# MILKMAN

# NURSE

Small white cap, shape varies with each hospital

Striped or spotted dress

White apron

A mop sewn on to a duster can be worn on the head

Plastic bucket

# MRS MOPP

# FISHERMAN

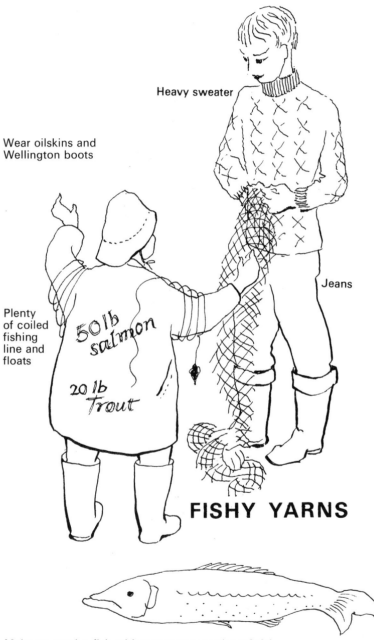

Heavy sweater

Wear oilskins and
Wellington boots

Jeans

Plenty
of coiled
fishing
line and
floats

50lb
salmon

20 lb
Trout

## FISHY YARNS

Make an outsize fish with newspaper papier mâché

# DAILY NEWS or CURRENT EVENTS

Cut out pieces of newspaper with bold headlines and sew them on to any old clothes

## SWEEP

Find dark clothes, an old cap and a black sack. Tie together a bundle of garden canes and borrow a flue or sweep's brush

# BALLOON SELLER

# FLOWER WOMAN

Lightweight shawl

Fill a tray with artificial flowers

Large coloured apron, not white

Avoid a floral material

# GIPSY

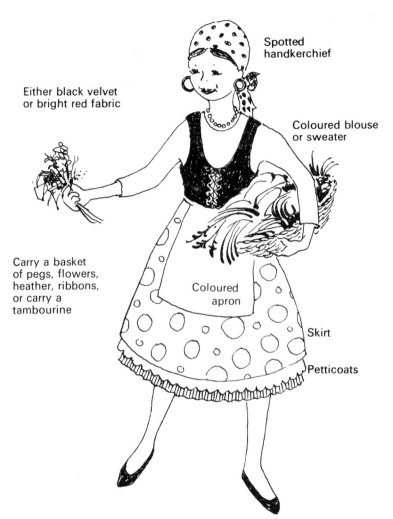

Spotted
handkerchief

Either black velvet
or bright red fabric

Coloured blouse
or sweater

Carry a basket
of pegs, flowers,
heather, ribbons,
or carry a
tambourine

Coloured
apron

Skirt

Petticoats

Wear several petticoats, as full as possible. Use bright rather garish
colours and some black, preferably bodice and shoes

# INDIAN BRAVE

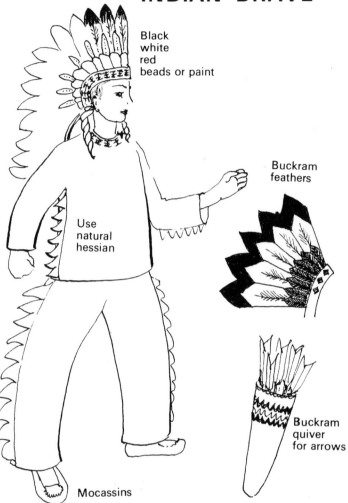

Black
white
red
beads or paint

Buckram
feathers

Use
natural
hessian

Buckram
quiver
for arrows

Mocassins

Set stiffly starched
coloured fabric
into the seams,
leave raw edges

Headband
Red, black,
pale blue

# and SQUAW

Black and white
turkey feather
stuck into centre
back of headband

Plush nylon and beads are
expensive. Instead use natural
hessian painted brick red,
turquoise, yellow ochre, with black
and white for contrast

Papoose,
a doll

Painted
panel

Fringe—use string
or cut the edge of
the material

Wear mocassins
and clumsy woollen
stockings or
suede boots

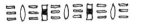

# COWBOY

Scarf tied to back or front

Hat can be worn either way

Check shirt

Cartridge belt

Rope

Usually 3 or eyelets

Wear jeans under chaps

High heeled boots; tuck jeans into top

Leather thongs or laces

Attach to jeans

Chaps must look like leather or furry cowhide. Use heavily starched brown hessian or two pieces of hessian with buckram between, all three pieces joined together with Copydex

# ESKIMO

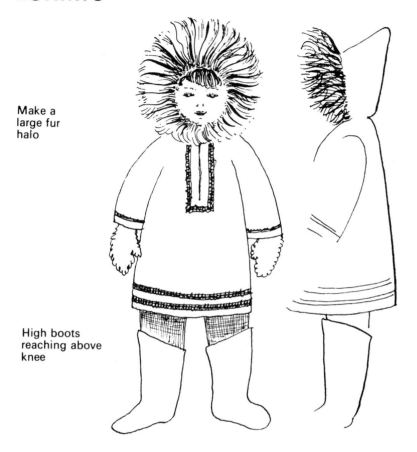

Make a
large fur
halo

High boots
reaching above
knee

The tunic is made of plain material imitating suede, with brightly
coloured red, blue, black and white bands. The general effect should
be of a very well-padded child therefore some foam rubber may be
necessary

# HAWAIAN

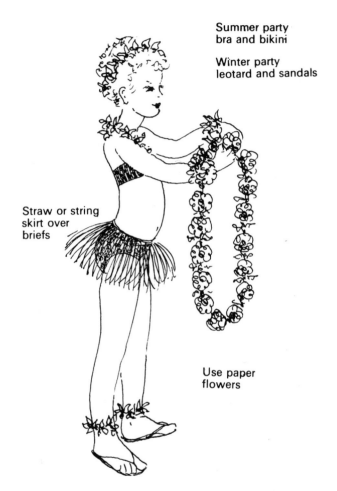

Summer party
bra and bikini

Winter party
leotard and sandals

Straw or string
skirt over
briefs

Use paper
flowers

Make flower ruffles for head, back, wrists and ankles and a big
garland to carry

# MEXICAN

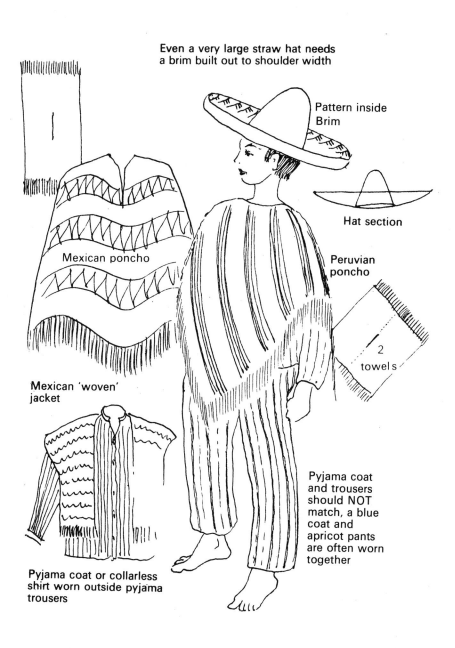

Even a very large straw hat needs a brim built out to shoulder width

Pattern inside Brim

Hat section

Mexican poncho

Peruvian poncho

2 towels

Mexican 'woven' jacket

Pyjama coat and trousers should NOT match, a blue coat and apricot pants are often worn together

Pyjama coat or collarless shirt worn outside pyjama trousers

# RAJAH

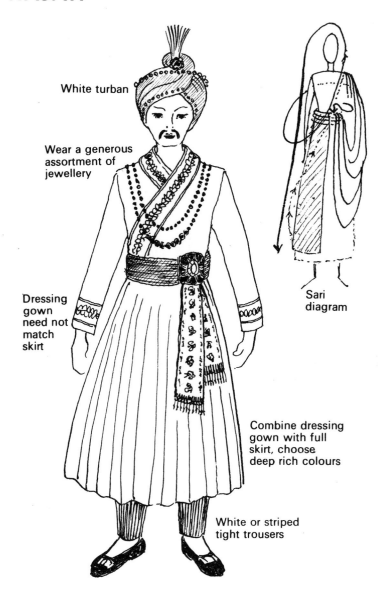

White turban

Wear a generous
assortment of
jewellery

Dressing
gown
need not
match
skirt

Sari
diagram

Combine dressing
gown with full
skirt, choose
deep rich colours

White or striped
tight trousers

# INDIAN WOMAN and RAJAH'S PAGE

A sari is 6 yards long, waist to ankle wide, tucks into a band and winds round the body and head

A shorter length of soft drapery is easier to arrange than 6 yards of sari

Each garment should be a different colour

Blouse, skirt and drapery need not match

# SHEIK

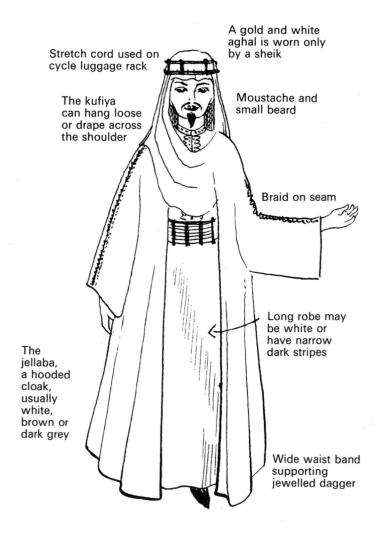

A gold and white aghal is worn only by a sheik

Stretch cord used on cycle luggage rack

The kufiya can hang loose or drape across the shoulder

Moustache and small beard

Braid on seam

The jellaba, a hooded cloak, usually white, brown or dark grey

Long robe may be white or have narrow dark stripes

Wide waist band supporting jewelled dagger

On a less important Arab the head band is black. The white cloth can be replaced with one which has a small close red or black pattern

# EUROPEAN GIPSY and SAHARAN GIRL

Make a loose bodice from dyed old sheet, paint the embroidery

Many necklaces

Gaily coloured sash

For both costumes choose many bright colours, pink, cerise, turquoise, and a variety of materials, dark velvet, plain, floral and stripes sateen

Long, full, but not transparent trousers

# EGYPTIAN WOMAN

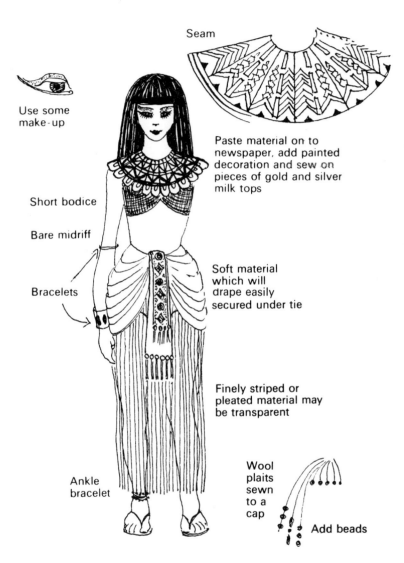

Seam

Use some make-up

Paste material on to newspaper, add painted decoration and sew on pieces of gold and silver milk tops

Short bodice

Bare midriff

Bracelets

Soft material which will drape easily secured under tie

Finely striped or pleated material may be transparent

Ankle bracelet

Wool plaits sewn to a cap

Add beads

A wig may have to be made or extra plaits added for effect. A dress for an older child

# PIERROT and CLOWN

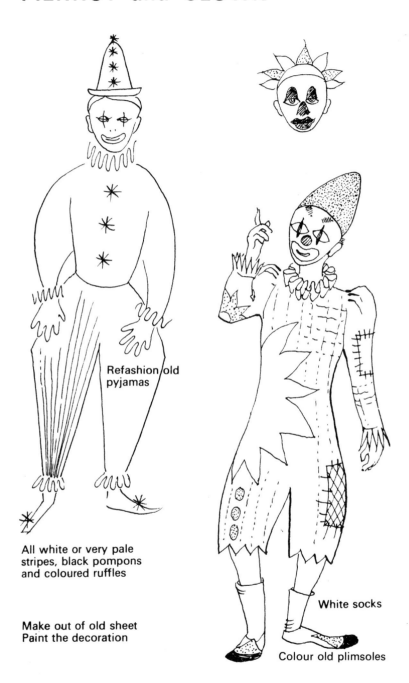

Refashion old
pyjamas

All white or very pale
stripes, black pompons
and coloured ruffles

Make out of old sheet
Paint the decoration

White socks

Colour old plimsoles

# BOOT'S BRANCHES

TONIC

TALC

TINCTURE

SERUM

PILLS

SOAP

POWDERS

TABLETS

Collect a variety of boots, all shapes and sizes. Label with suitable captions, attach to wire or small branches secured to pads on the shoulders. Wire must be stout enough to support the weight of the boots

Alternative— tie boots to large pliant twigs

Shoes will not do instead of boots

# KNIGHT OF THE BATH

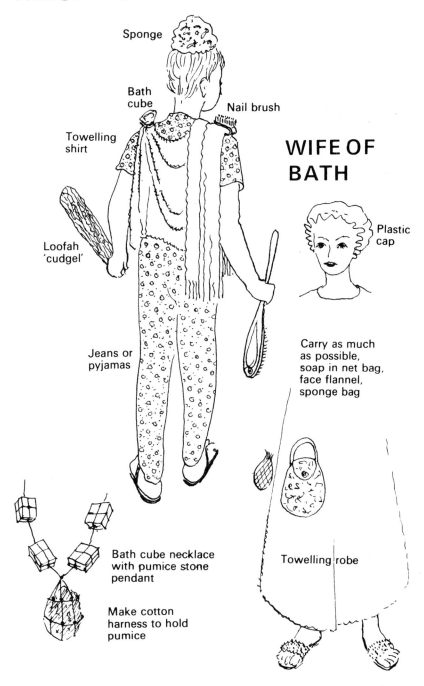

Sponge

Bath cube

Nail brush

Towelling shirt

**WIFE OF BATH**

Plastic cap

Loofah 'cudgel'

Jeans or pyjamas

Carry as much as possible, soap in net bag, face flannel, sponge bag

Bath cube necklace with pumice stone pendant

Make cotton harness to hold pumice

Towelling robe

# BOXED GOODS

Sugar bag

Fruit-nut bar

Frozen foods

Chocolate bar

Luggage

Duffle bag

Daily paper

Catalogue

Mis(s)print

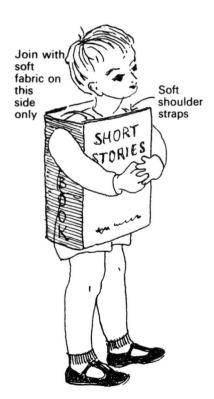

Join with soft fabric on this side only

Soft shoulder straps

Paint a piece of old sheet

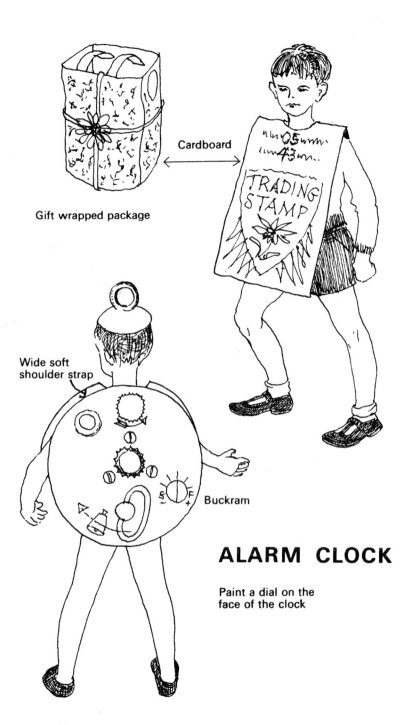

Gift wrapped package

Cardboard

Wide soft
shoulder strap

Buckram

## ALARM CLOCK

Paint a dial on the
face of the clock

# PLAYING CARDS

## QUEEN OF HEARTS

Under playing card
wear red tunic and
white tights or
black tunic and red
tights

Red, with
white lines

This could be a group
or family entry to a
competition

# JACK OF DIAMONDS

Red

Shoes
red or black

Red, with
black lines

# JACK OF CLUBS

Adapt designs from
playing cards
Paint in red, black,
royal blue and yellow
on thick white card

Yellow
with red
and black
pattern

Black
tights

Dark
blue shoes

# KING OF SPADES

Black tights

Royal blue
shoes

# CHRISTMAS CRACKER

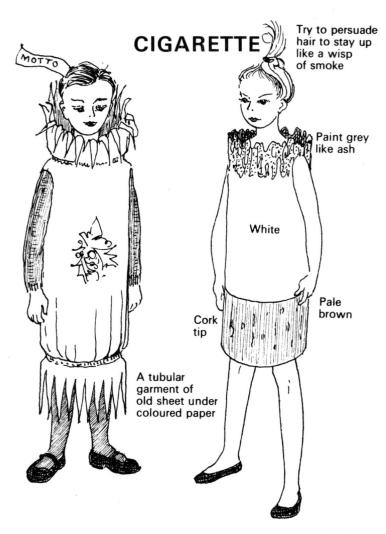

CIGARETTE

Try to persuade hair to stay up like a wisp of smoke

MOTTO

Paint grey like ash

White

A tubular garment of old sheet under coloured paper

Cork tip

Pale brown

Make cracker with crêpe paper gathered on to elastic so that there is reasonable movement during games when the skirt can be lifted. The cigarette must either have a slit at each side or be cut short enough to enable easy movement

# BELISHA BEACON

## ZEBRA CROSSING

Use a lampshade painted orange.

Fix over hair dressed in a bun on top of head

Cut a full length straight dress. Paint stripes on sleeves to match those on body

If a lampshade head-dress is too difficult to secure, an orange woollen hat could be used, though this would be hotter to wear

Cut to allow movement

# DUSTBIN                    PILLAR BOX

Hinge the lid
and support it
at each side

Show some old
cartons and paper
bags which must
be light weight and
firmly attached

Corrugated
paper painted
grey

Make.cut in card
wide enough not
to pinch the arm.
Leave slit in
covering fabric

Hang by
shoulder straps
stapled to
back and front
of dustbin

Removable lid

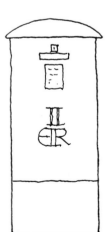

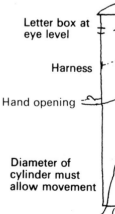

Letter box at
eye level

Harness

Hand opening

Diameter of
cylinder must
allow movement

# COTTAGE LOAF

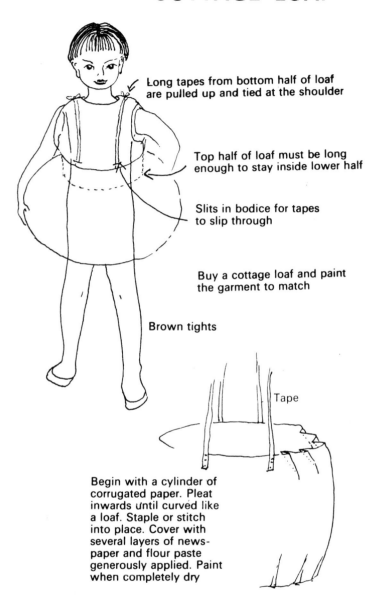

Long tapes from bottom half of loaf are pulled up and tied at the shoulder

Top half of loaf must be long enough to stay inside lower half

Slits in bodice for tapes to slip through

Buy a cottage loaf and paint the garment to match

Brown tights

Tape

Begin with a cylinder of corrugated paper. Pleat inwards until curved like a loaf. Staple or stitch into place. Cover with several layers of newspaper and flour paste generously applied. Paint when completely dry

# SAUCEPAN, ON THE BOIL
## or BOILING OVER

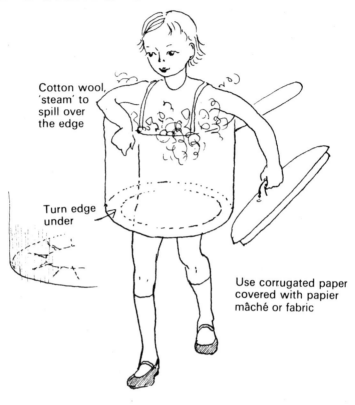

Cotton wool, 'steam' to spill over the edge

Turn edge under

Use corrugated paper covered with papier mâché or fabric

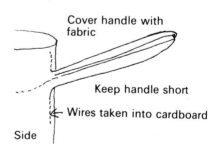

Cover handle with fabric

Keep handle short

Wires taken into cardboard

Side

This can be worn by a very plump child.

# CUP OF TEA

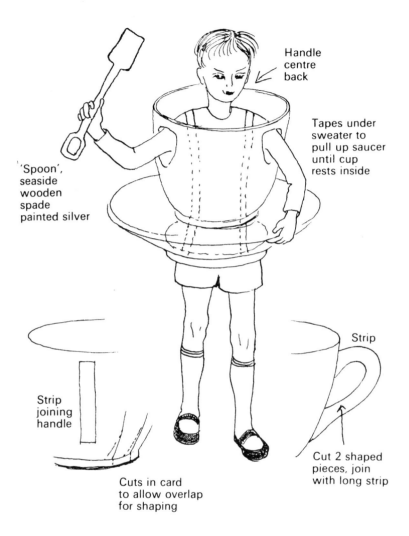

Handle centre back

Tapes under sweater to pull up saucer until cup rests inside

'Spoon', seaside wooden spade painted silver

Strip

Strip joining handle

Cut 2 shaped pieces, join with long strip

Cuts in card to allow overlap for shaping

This costume is easier to fit on a child with narrow hips otherwise the base of the cup becomes too wide

# EASTER EGG

Head should pass through easily with just enough shoulder strap to balance

Soft near opening

Soft beneath ribbon for flexibility

Make a hole large enough to allow free movement

HAPPY EASTER

Built on a corrugated paper frame with some wire for support. This must be kept as light weight as possible yet remain firm.
Cover with plain paper or newspaper. Paint any colour. Make a crêpe paper bow

# SNOWMAN

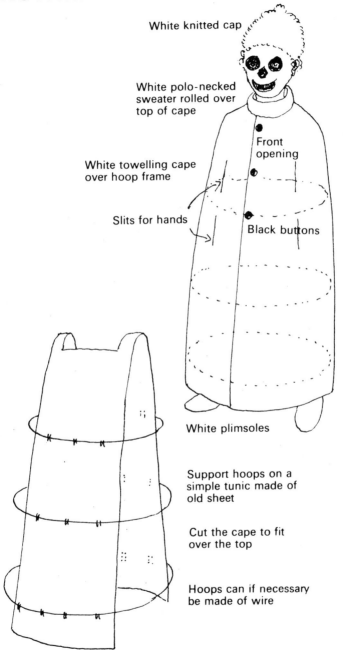

White knitted cap

White polo-necked sweater rolled over top of cape

White towelling cape over hoop frame

Slits for hands

Front opening

Black buttons

White plimsoles

Support hoops on a simple tunic made of old sheet

Cut the cape to fit over the top

Hoops can if necessary be made of wire

# BIRD TABLE

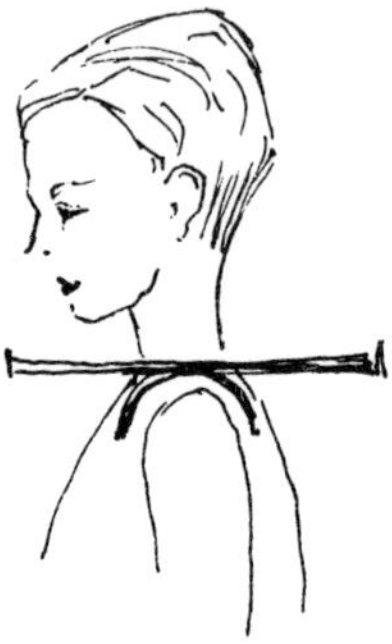

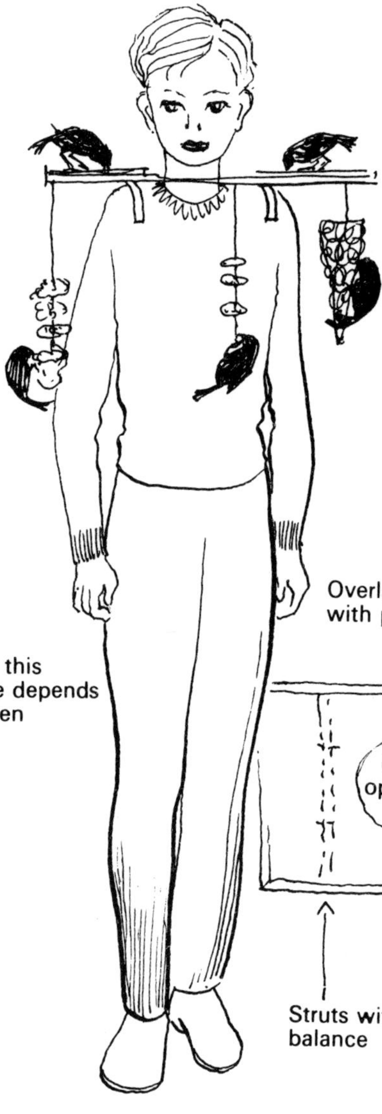

The success of this
simple costume depends
on the care taken
to model each
bird accurately

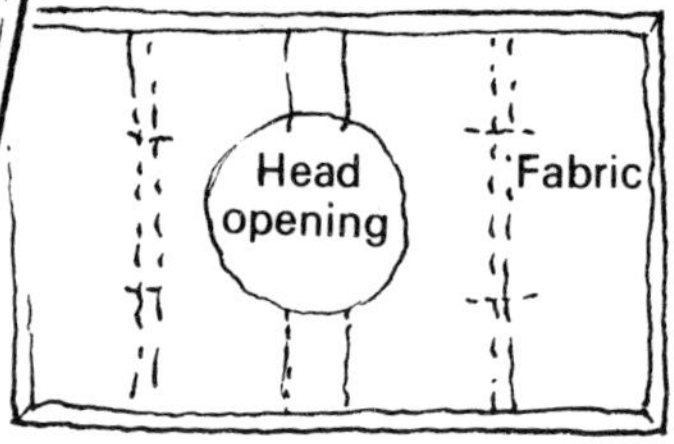

Overlapping fabric
with press studs

Head
opening

Fabric

Frame

Struts with shoulder
balance

# SKELETON

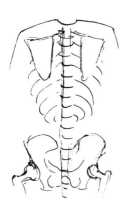

Back view

Head—use a
black balaclava
with make up on
the face or wear
a painted mask

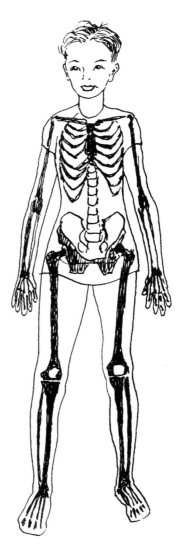

Although the diagram
shows black on white, use
a black leotard or sweater and
tights, gloves and
shoes with a white
painted skeleton

# CAT

# RABBIT

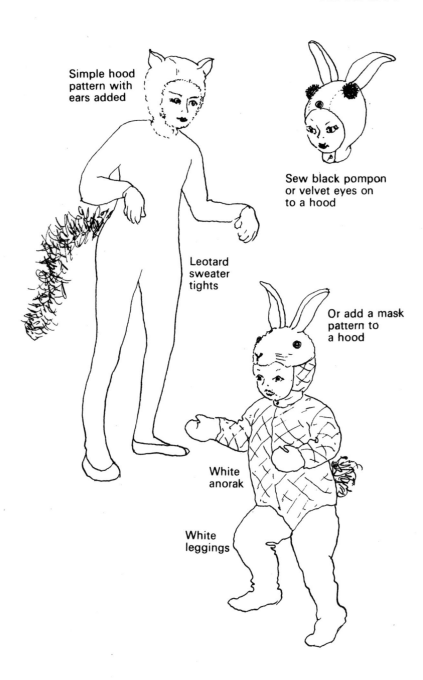

Simple hood pattern with ears added

Sew black pompon or velvet eyes on to a hood

Leotard sweater tights

Or add a mask pattern to a hood

White anorak

White leggings

# POODLE

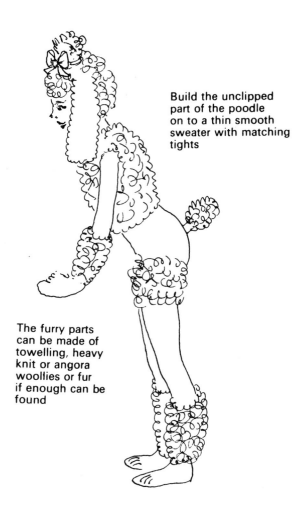

Build the unclipped
part of the poodle
on to a thin smooth
sweater with matching
tights

The furry parts
can be made of
towelling, heavy
knit or angora
woollies or fur
if enough can be
found

# BIRD MASKS designed by Linda Cole

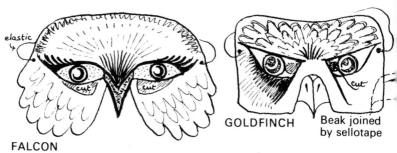

elastic

FALCON

GOLDFINCH | Beak joined by sellotape

Cut out of cardboard, coloured
with paint, felt pen and wax
crayon. Tied with hat elastic

Eye opening

OWL

Animal masks can be made in the same way  See also page 96

A bird or animal mask can easily become the most complicated part
of a costume. Three methods are shown, a very simple paper mask,
a cap mask and a hood mask in which the child's face comes between
the animal's jaws. Any mask is hot to wear; for this reason the cap
and hood varieties may be fitted on a cotton bonnet but never upon
a rubber bathing cap

The wings need stiffening but should not be rigid. One piece of
Staflex is enough and this can be coloured with a felt pen or placed
between 2 pieces of painted material

# WINGS and       TAILS

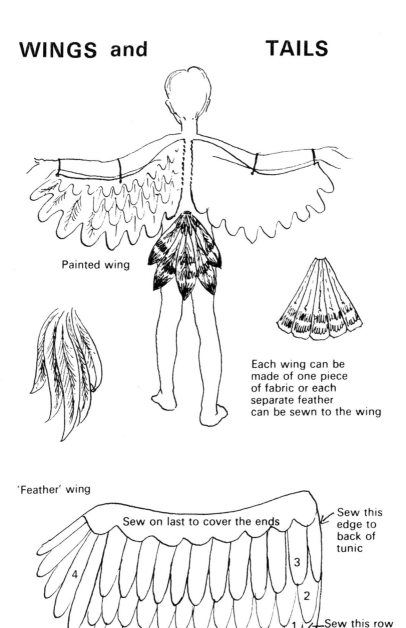

Painted wing

Each wing can be
made of one piece
of fabric or each
separate feather
can be sewn to the wing

'Feather' wing

Sew on last to cover the ends

Sew this
edge to
back of
tunic

4

3

2

1

Sew this row
on first

# COCK

Bottle green
sweater with
extra feather
skirt or make
a tunic

Fit wings for
cock and hen in
the same way

Spurs made
from leather or
plastic belt

Build cock's head on a cotton cap. Make beak, eyes and comb of
felt and the feathers of stiffened material. Wire the tail feathers
between two pieces of stiffened material. Add painted decoration.

# HEN

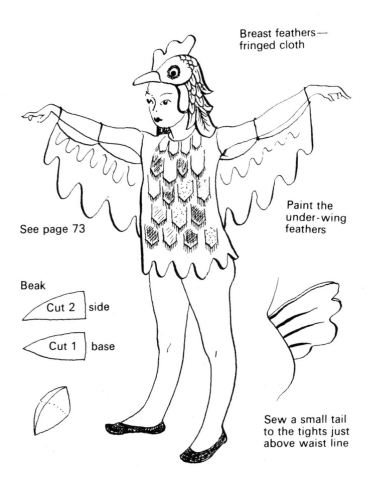

Breast feathers—
fringed cloth

Paint the
under-wing
feathers

See page 73

Beak

Cut 2 | side

Cut 1 | base

Sew a small tail
to the tights just
above waist line

A sunbonnet is a useful foundation for the head-dress which can be
made of coloured material sewn on to it, with felt used for comb,
beak and eyes

# DRAGON

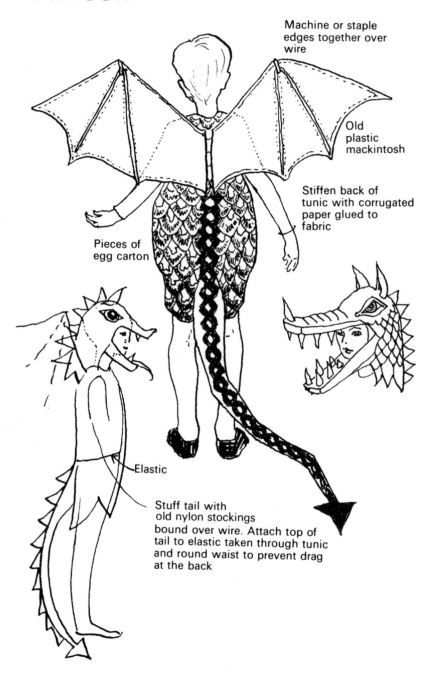

Machine or staple edges together over wire

Old plastic mackintosh

Stiffen back of tunic with corrugated paper glued to fabric

Pieces of egg carton

Elastic

Stuff tail with old nylon stockings bound over wire. Attach top of tail to elastic taken through tunic and round waist to prevent drag at the back

# CROCODILE

Interchangeable
head construction for
crocodile and dragon
Adapt pattern on page 96

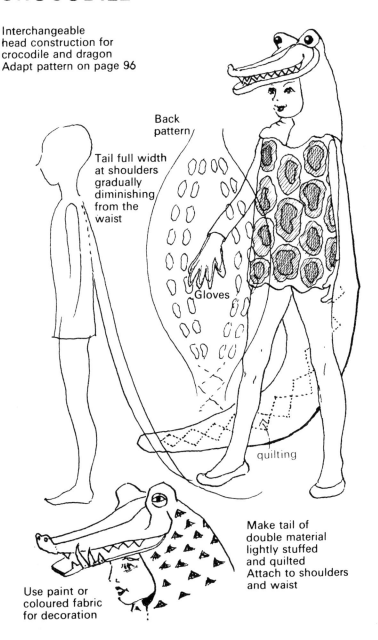

Back
pattern

Tail full width
at shoulders
gradually
diminishing
from the
waist

Gloves

quilting

Make tail of
double material
lightly stuffed
and quilted
Attach to shoulders
and waist

Use paint or
coloured fabric
for decoration

# TREE TRUNK

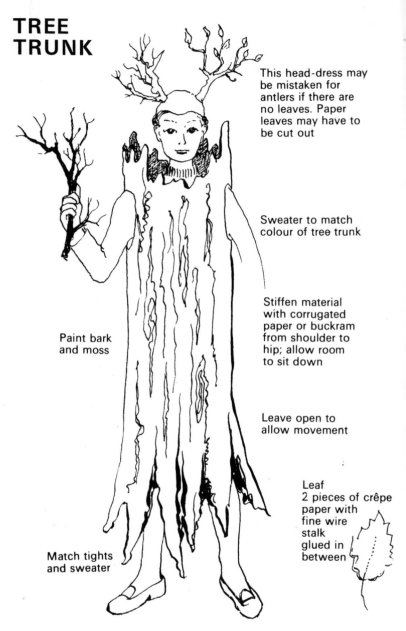

This head-dress may be mistaken for antlers if there are no leaves. Paper leaves may have to be cut out

Sweater to match colour of tree trunk

Stiffen material with corrugated paper or buckram from shoulder to hip; allow room to sit down

Leave open to allow movement

Leaf
2 pieces of crêpe paper with fine wire stalk glued in between

Paint bark and moss

Match tights and sweater

Choose a tree with a distinctive bark pattern such as pine, silver birch or oak. Make sure that the leaves match. For a pine tree omit the head-dress

# EARS OF CORN

Crown of corn

Harvest mouse, brown pompons, felt ears and a pipe-cleaner tail

Yellow sweater or bare arms

If possible sew real ears of corn among the painted patterns

Yellow tights

Brown shoes

Skirt length unimportant. Legs should be nearly straw colour to represent the cornstalk

# CRAB

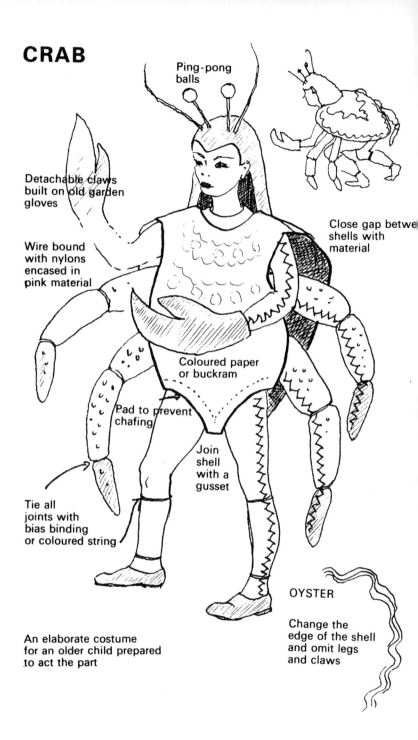

Ping-pong balls

Detachable claws built on old garden gloves

Wire bound with nylons encased in pink material

Close gap between shells with material

Coloured paper or buckram

Pad to prevent chafing

Join shell with a gusset

Tie all joints with bias binding or coloured string

An elaborate costume for an older child prepared to act the part

OYSTER

Change the edge of the shell and omit legs and claws

# HATCHING CHICK

Wear a yellow cap and
blouse, white knickers
and yellow tights
Red shoes match the beak

Stiffen top edge with
Vilene or Staflex

Add a piece of white
material to knickers
There is no need to alter
strap position

# BUMBLEBEE

# WASP

Make garment
with zip down
centre back.
Sew wings on
either side

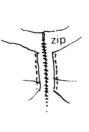

zip

For a bee
black velvet

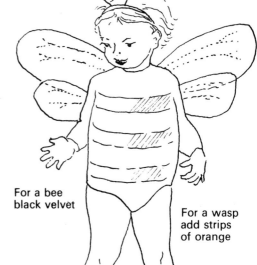

For a wasp
add strips
of orange

To be worn bare
legged or with
coloured tights;
socks spoil the
effect

# BUTTERFLY

# BUTTERFLY

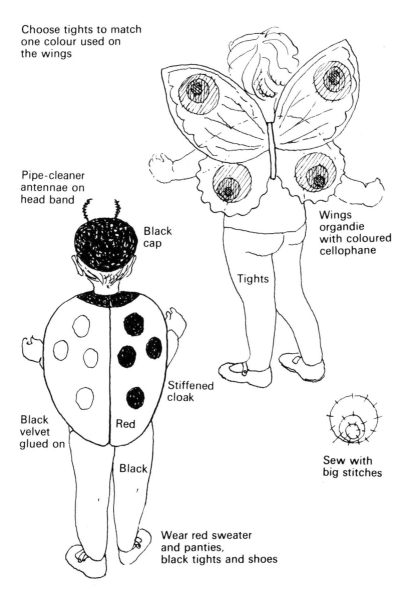

Choose tights to match one colour used on the wings

Pipe-cleaner antennae on head band

Black cap

Wings organdie with coloured cellophane

Tights

Stiffened cloak

Black velvet glued on

Red

Black

Sew with big stitches

Wear red sweater and panties, black tights and shoes

# LADYBIRD or BEETLE

# ROSEBUD

Back view of wild rose
cut from Vilene and
coloured with felt pens

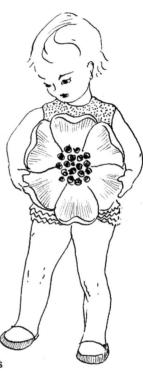

Vilene rose joined to
front of tunic.
Coloured with felt
tipped pens, or paint,
or coloured wax crayons

Daisy flowers
edging yoke

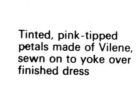

Tinted, pink-tipped
petals made of Vilene,
sewn on to yoke over
finished dress

## DAISY

# LIMPET

Make a cone-shaped
dress lined with Staflex.
Cover outside with
Vilene and paint the
limpet pattern

Tunic, turquoise fabric
with pieces of green
plastic and brown if
available. Attach small
shells with Bostick

# SEAWEED

Wear a sea anemone in the hair
or on one shoulder. Make it
with crêpe paper or use a
coloured powder puff on
a felt stalk

# THE SEASONS

## SPRING

Chiefly shades of green and yellow.
Sew buttercups, daisies, violets
and celandines on a plain
summer dress

## SUMMER

Wild roses, honeysuckle,
pansies, marguerites,
and seeding grass. Use
iron on Staflex coloured with
felt pens.

Staple
cut out paper petals on to a
piece of tape; tie under chin

# AUTUMN

Black berries,
crab apples,
heather, bracken,
brown curled leaves or
leaves flattened and
varnished. Oiled leaves
are flexible

Tunic—russet coloured

# WINTER

Either cold blue with tufts of cotton wool snow, white Christmas
roses and yellow winter jasmine; pale blue stockings
or
bright red tunic with white Christmas roses and imitation holly and
mistletoe cut out of Staflex or Vilene—all detail added with felt pen

# RAIN   WATER

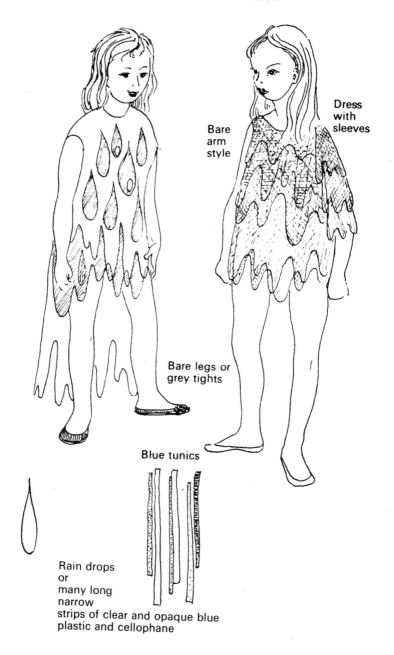

Dress with sleeves

Bare arm style

Bare legs or grey tights

Blue tunics

Rain drops
or
many long
narrow
strips of clear and opaque blue
plastic and cellophane

# FIRE

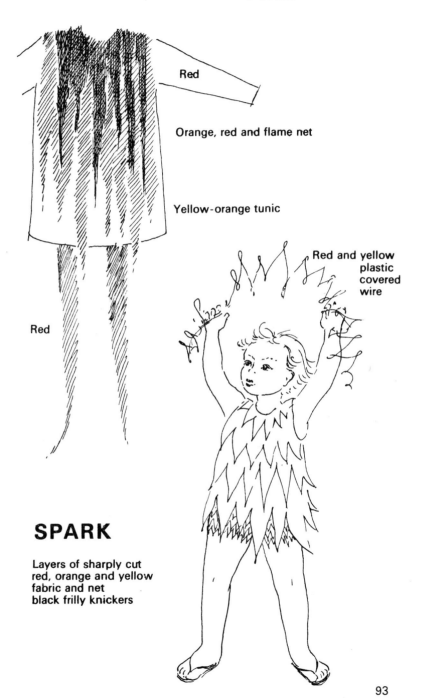

Red

Orange, red and flame net

Yellow-orange tunic

Red

Red and yellow plastic covered wire

## SPARK

Layers of sharply cut red, orange and yellow fabric and net black frilly knickers

# NIGHT AND DAY

Make tunic blue in front with a
great golden sun covering most of
it. Make the back dark blue with
silver stars and a pale yellow
moon

or

wear a black sweater and tights
with similar decoration applied
with fairly loose hemming so that
the garment is not damaged when
the motifs are removed

# NIGHT

Soft blue tunic covered with layers of different shades of blue net cut unevenly with large curved edges. Sew on moon and stars made from cooking foil. The moon can show through clouds cut from a plastic bag or wrapper

Stars joined to head band with cotton and an adhesive

Bare arms and legs for a summer party, tights for the winter

# ANIMAL HEAD Cap style

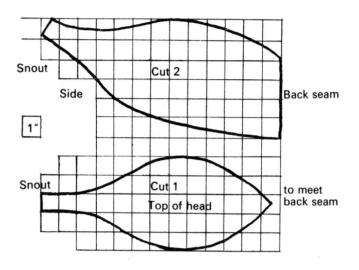

Snout

Cut 2

Side

Back seam

1"

Snout

Cut 1

Top of head

to meet
back seam

Eye position

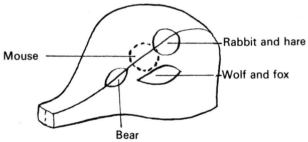

Mouse

Rabbit and hare

Wolf and fox

Bear

Use animal photographs to give the exact eye position. Test by
moving a piece of paper until the right expression is found. Find the
ear position in the same way